180 Days
Cursive
Beginning

Publishing Credits

Corinne Burton, M.A.Ed., *Publisher*
Emily R. Smith, M.A.Ed., *Senior VP of Content Development*
Véronique Bos, *Vice President of Creative*
Andrew Greene, M.A.Ed., *Senior Content Manager*
Jill Malcolm, *Graphic Designer*

Standards

Image Credits: all images from iStock and/or Shutterstock

A division of Teacher Created Materials
5482 Argosy Avenue
Huntington Beach, CA 92649
www.tcmpub.com/shell-education
ISBN 978-1-0876-6243-5
© 2023 Shell Educational Publishing, Inc.
Printed in USA. WOR004

Table of Contents

Introduction

Weekly Practice Pages

Table of Contents *(cont.)*

Weekly Practice Pages

Appendix

Foundations for Cursive

Welcome to *180 Days of Cursive: Beginning*! Students will learn the foundations for writing in cursive, including strokes and connections. They will learn not only how to form individual letters, but also how to make connections between letters to write words and sentences. These practice pages provide engaging ways for young learners to develop good handwriting habits.

Hand-eye Coordination

Hand-eye coordination is essential for handwriting. Students track lines with their eyes to guide, direct, and control hand movement. Coordination allows students to write on the line, properly space letters, write proper letter size, and more. This developmental approach is also seen in research-based programs, such as Handwriting Without Tears. Hand-eye coordination is reinforced throughout this book through engaging, age-appropriate activities and practice pages.

Drawing

Drawing helps students develop fine-motor skills that extend to handwriting, such as holding a writing instrument correctly and applying the correct amount of force and speed to mark paper. Just as with print, students benefit from drawing as a way to build motor control in a fun and engaging manner. Drawing keeps writers engaged through fun activities and practice pages.

Tracing

Tracing reinforces basic stroke formation along with hand-eye coordination. As a fine-tuning skill, tracing helps students develop fine-motor skills as they practice cursive. Students also become more aware of spacing, which is essential for writing well in cursive.

Getting Ready to Write

Pencil Grip

Students will naturally find their dominant hand as they learn to properly grip writing instruments. Help students decide which hand is more comfortable to write with, and guide them to alternate hands if they show no clear preference. Teach students a pencil grip with their pointer finger on the top, thumb on the side, and three fingers below the pencil to support the grip. Encourage students to use this pencil grip as they work through the pages of the book.

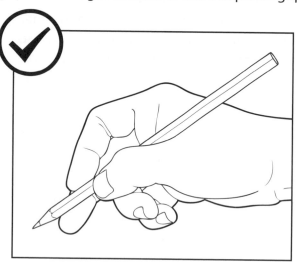
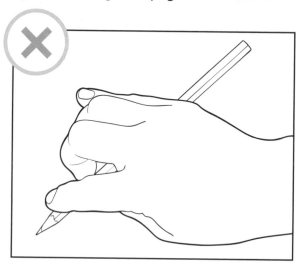

Pencil Weight (Writing Too Hard or Too Soft)

Students should press down on the pencil with medium weight. Demonstrate the proper pressure to use when writing—not too hard and not too soft. Bring students' attention to the color of the line when the correct weight is used.

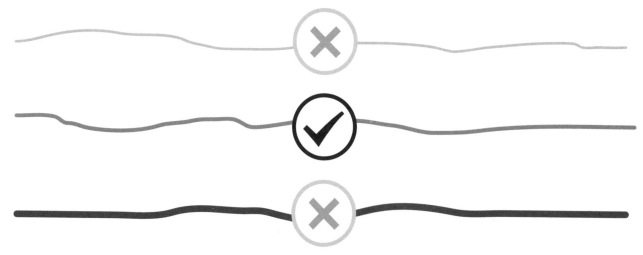

Letter Spacing

Teach students proper letter spacing within a word and between words in a sentence. While cursive letters within a word connect, each letter should be defined and each connecting stroke should form a cohesive transition. As students grasp spacing within words, demonstrate the required spacing between words. Remind students that there should be no connecting strokes between words, and that there should be a space just like when printing. Reinforce letter spacing as students practice writing sentences on the review pages.

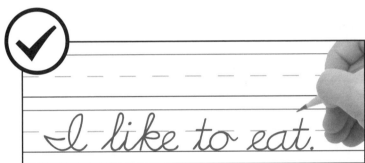

Letter Angle

Cursive should be written at a slight angle. Demonstrate writing at a slope for students to observe and encourage them to match the angle of the letters. Show students how to hold the page at an angle with their nondominant hand to help create the proper letter shapes. Encourage students to try different ways of holding the page to find the most comfortable position for writing—left-handed and right-handed students may benefit from holding the book at different angles as they write.

Letter Presentation Order

To give students a strong foundation in handwriting, this book builds off the smallest handwriting units—strokes. By presenting letters by strokes used for cursive letters instead of alphabetical order, students can more easily make connections on how to write them. The letter presentation order also takes into account whether the letter is formed with a stroke from the top or bottom. Presenting letters by stroke also gives students ample practice time to create and refine motor control when creating letter strokes. The use of repetition in presenting strokes across multiple weeks provides the practice young learners need to increase proficiency.

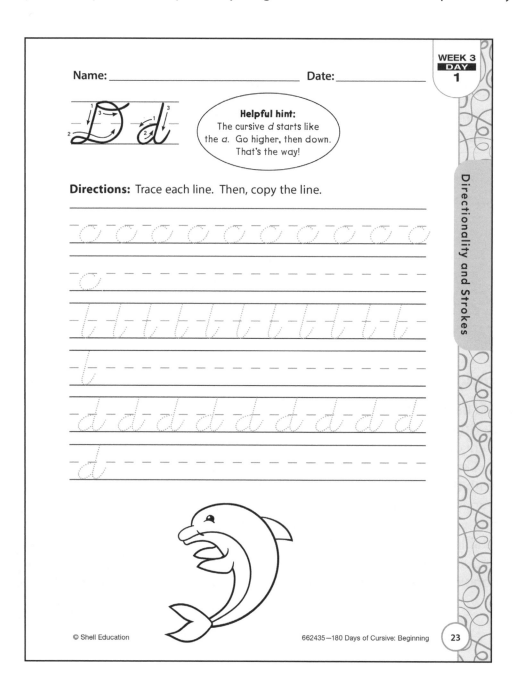

Sight Words

This program takes a holistic approach to handwriting, teaching not only individual letters but also how they fit into words and sentences. High-frequency words pulled from Dr. Edward Fry's Instant Words list and Dr. Edward Dolch's Most Common Words list allow students to practice words they will see and write frequently. The use of these sight words to practice handwriting increases letter awareness as students are exposed to these letters and words in other age-appropriate learning materials.

How to Use This Book

Day 1

Directionality and Strokes

180 Days of Cursive: Beginning prioritizes giving students a strong foundation. Before each letter is introduced, students have a chance to practice strokes—the basic shapes that make up letters. Students practice the individual strokes of the lowercase and uppercase letter before applying all the strokes to write.

Day 2

Cursive Lowercase

Lowercase letters are introduced after the relevant letter strokes are introduced and practiced, setting students up for success. Students benefit from tracing letters, writing letters independently, and writing letters as parts of words. Students begin understanding letter shapes, spacing, and connection. They are also exposed to vocabulary and sight words.

Day 3

Cursive Uppercase

Uppercase letters are introduced after lowercase letters, continuing to build on relevant strokes. Students benefit from tracing letters, writing letters independently, and writing letters as parts of words. Students practice letter shapes, spacing, and connections as they write proper nouns.

Day 4

Activity

Activities give students opportunities to practice strokes, directionality, and letter recognition in engaging ways. At the beginning level of cursive, it is important to focus on refining fine-motor skills and making practice fun.

Day 5

Review

A key to mastering cursive is repetition. Weekly reviews provide students with extra practice. The reviews help students move towards more independent writing. The reviews also provide opportunities to practice sight words through repetition.

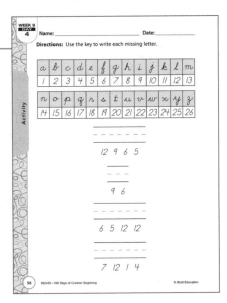

Standards Correlations

Shell Education is committed to producing educational materials that are research and standards based. To support this effort, this resource is correlated to the academic standards of all 50 states, the District of Columbia, the Department of Defense Dependent Schools, and the Canadian provinces. A correlation is also provided for key professional educational organizations.

To print a customized correlation report for your state, please visit our website at **www.tcmpub.com/administrators/correlations** and follow the online directions. If you require assistance in printing correlation reports, please contact the Customer Service Department at 1-800-858-7339.

Stroke and Directionality (Day 1)	**Foundational Skills: Adjust grasp and body position for increased control in drawing and writing.** • Demonstrate proper finger grasp. • Begin using nondominant hand to hold paper to maintain control.
Cursive Lowercase (Day 2)	**Foundational Skills: Print all upper- and lowercase letters.** • Recognize and print all upper- and lowercase letters of the alphabet. **Foundational Skills: Capitalize dates and names of people.** • Demonstrate understanding of capitalization. **Foundational Skills: Capitalize holidays, product names, and geographic names.** • Demonstrate understanding of capitalization.
Cursive Uppercase (Day 3)	**Foundational Skills: Capitalize appropriate words.** • Demonstrate understanding of the organization and basic features of print.
Activity (Day 4)	**Foundational Skills: Practice words phonetically, drawing on phonemic awareness and spelling conventions.** • Demonstrate the ability to decode new vocabulary through phonemic and spelling awareness.
Review (Day 5)	**Foundational Skills: Use frequently occurring nouns and verbs.** • Begin reading and writing high-frequency nouns and verbs. • Demonstrate basic comprehension of nouns and verbs through sight words.

Name: _____ **Date:** _____

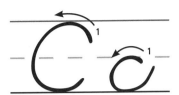

Directions: Trace the curves. Then, copy each row.

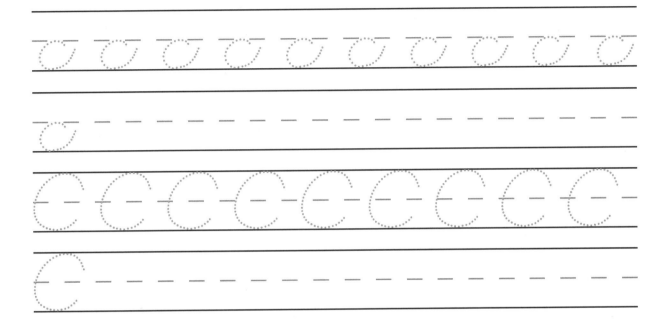

Directions: Trace each curve. Practice writing each curve without lifting your pencil.

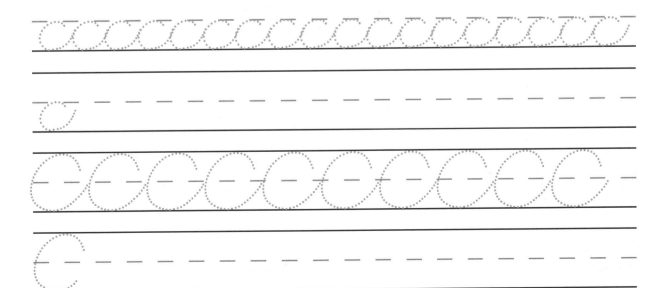

Name: _____   Date: _____

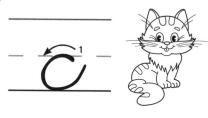

Directions: Trace each letter c. Then, practice writing and connecting the letters.

Cursive Lowercase

Directions: Trace each letter to finish the words.

cat

fact

back

chair

© Shell Education

Name: _____ **Date:** _____

Directions: Trace each letter. Then, practice writing the letter.

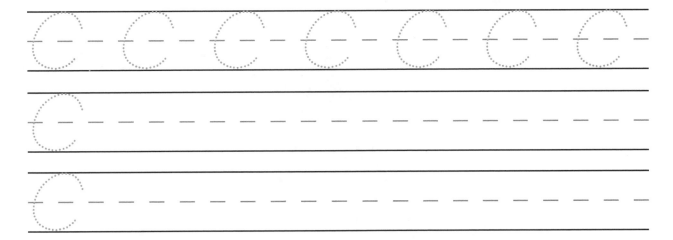

Directions: Trace each letter to finish the names.

Carmen

Carmen

Clayton

Clayton

Colorado

Colorado

Clara

Clara

Name: _____ **Date:** _____

Directions: Trace the curves. Then, color the page.

Activity

Name: _____ **Date:** _____

Directions: Trace each letter. Then, write the letters to fill the lines.

Directions: Trace each letter. Then, write the missing letters to complete the words.

arry   *arry*

whi h   *whi h*

Name: _____ **Date:** _____

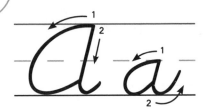

Helpful hint: The cursive *a* starts like the *c*. Come back up to close the letter. It's as easy as can be!

Directions: Trace the curves and letters. Then, copy each row.

Name: _____ Date: _____

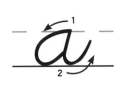 

Directions: Trace each letter. Then, practice writing and connecting the letters.

a a a a a a a a a a

a

a a

a a a

Directions: Trace each letter to finish the words.

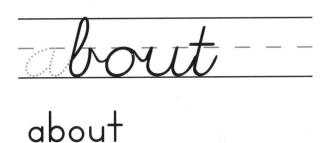

around

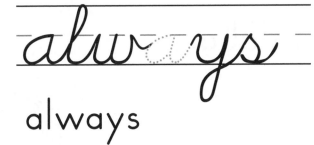

read

about

always

Name: _____ Date: _____

𝒶

Directions: Trace each letter. Then, practice writing the letter.

_𝒶_ _𝒶_ _𝒶_ _𝒶_ _𝒶_ _𝒶_ _𝒶_

_𝒶_

_𝒶_

Directions: Trace each letter to finish the names.

𝒜isha

Aisha

𝒜hmed

Ahmed

𝒜labama

Alabama

𝒜lyssa

Alyssa

Name: _____ **Date:** _____

Directions: Fill in the missing letters.

What has two hands but cannot scratch itself?

$$a \quad \underline{o}$$

What do you call a cat crossed with a fish?

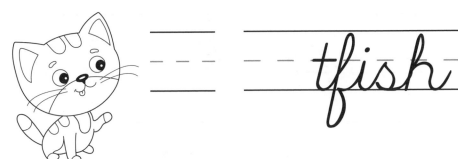

What is orange, green on top, and rhymes with parrot?

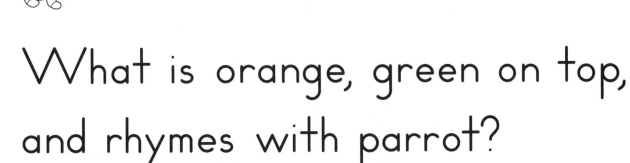

Name: _____   Date: _____

Directions: Trace each letter.

_____

o o o o o o o o o o o o

c c c c c c c c

_____

a a a a a a a a a

a a a a a a a

Directions: Trace each letter. Then, write the missing letters to complete the words.

pi k   pi k

wash   w sh

Review

Name: _____   **Date:** _____

Helpful hint:
The cursive *d* starts like
the *a*. Go higher, then down.
That's the way!

Directions: Trace the curves and letters. Then, copy each row.

Name: _____ **Date:** _____

Cursive Lowercase

Directions: Trace each letter. Then, practice writing and connecting the letters.

Directions: Trace each letter to finish the words.

does

found

draw

hold

130195—180 Days of Cursive: Beginning

Name: _____ **Date:** _____

Directions: Trace each letter. Then, practice writing the letter.

Directions: Trace each letter to finish the names.

Doug

Dalilah

Darcy

Deshaun

Name: _____ **Date:** _____

Directions: Find and circle the listed words.

d x u s h e x e g k
i r a u m c j a n i
t b o a o a v d c h
d x u f u t i d s n
w s j q p p d y u e
l i l m z l a i g i
v e o u b z d z e n
c c t n q j x j a y
s s y v l x j v c t
c a p z e x k e t g

act add cap cat dad

Name: _____   Date: _____

Directions: Trace each letter. Then, write the letters to fill the lines.

_____

o o o o _____

c c c _____

a a a a _____

d d d _____

d d d d _____

B B B _____

Directions: Trace each letter. Then, write the missing letters to complete the words.

_____

arry   *arry*

back   *b ck*

di   *i*

Name: _____ Date: _____

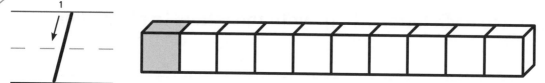

Directions: Trace the number. Then, practice writing 1 on the lines.

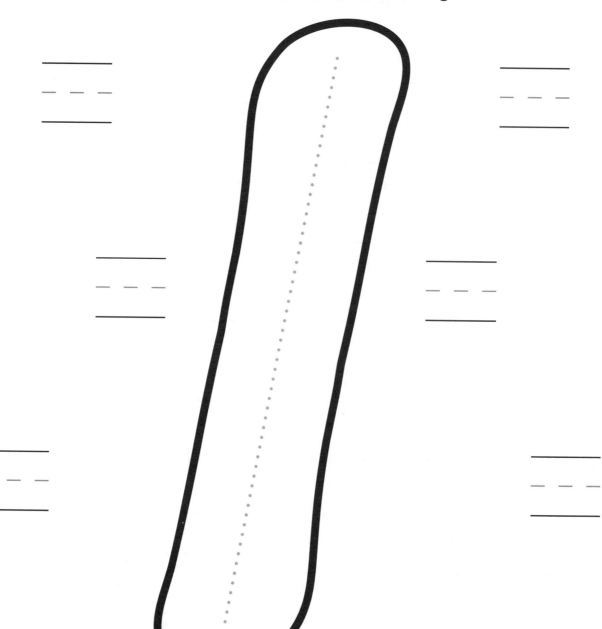

Name: _____   **Date:** _____

Directions: Trace each number. Then, practice writing the numbers.

0 _____   5 _____

_____   6 _____

2 _____   7 _____

3 _____   8 _____

4 _____   9 _____

Numbers

Name: _____ **Date:** _____

Directions: Count how many things you see. Then, write the numbers on the lines.

There are
_____
_ _ _ _
_____ *cubes.*

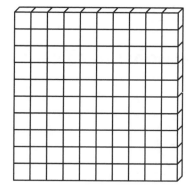

There are
_____
_ _ _ _
_____ *apples.*

There is
_____
_ _ _ _
_____ *bike.*

I have
_____
_ _ _ _
_____ *cents.*

Name: _____ **Date:** _____

Directions: Use the key to match the letters to the numbers. Write each missing letter. Then, write the words in cursive.

a	b	c	d	e	f	g	h	i	j	k	l	m
1	2	3	4	5	6	7	8	9	10	11	12	13

n	o	p	q	r	s	t	u	v	w	x	y	z
14	15	16	17	18	19	20	21	22	23	24	25	26

t

3 1 20

og

4 15 7

u k

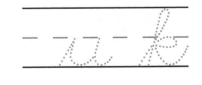

4 21 3 11

Name: _____ Date: _____

Directions: Trace each letter. Then, write the letters to fill the lines.

Directions: Trace each letter. Then, write the missing letters to complete the words.

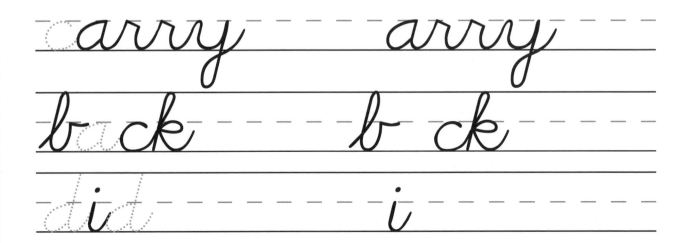

Name: _____ Date: _____

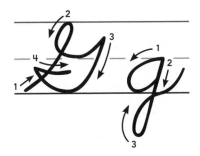

Directions: Trace the curves and loops. Then, copy each row.

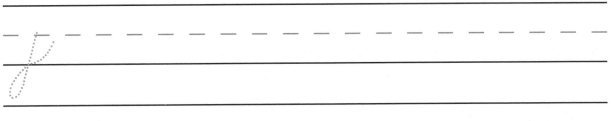

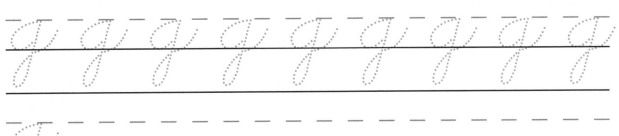

Name: _____   Date: _____

Helpful hint:
The cursive *g* starts like the *a*.
Loop down, then around.
That's the way!

Cursive Lowercase

Directions: Trace each letter. Then, practice writing and connecting the letters.

g   g   g   g   g   g   g   g   g   g

g

gg

Directions: Trace each letter to finish the words.

gave

gave

laugh

laugh

green

green

young

young

Name: _____ Date: _____

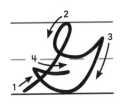 

Directions: Trace each letter. Then, practice writing the letter.

Directions: Trace each letter to finish the names.

Gary

Gary

Grace

Grace

Georgia

Georgia

Glenn

Glenn

130195—180 Days of Cursive: Beginning

Name: _____ Date: _____

Directions: Unscramble the letters. Then, write the words in cursive.

Clue: *Fruits and vegetables*

rrocta

_____ arrot

eprag

r pe

ronage

or n e

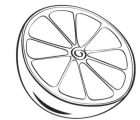

pplea

pple

alek

k le

annaab

b n n

Name: _____ **Date:** _____

Directions: Trace each letter. Then, write the letters to fill the lines.

a a a a

a a a

d d d d

D D D

g g g g

y y y

Directions: Trace each letter. Then, write the missing letters to complete the words.

arry   *arry*

kin   *kin*

page   *pa e*

Name: _____ Date: _____

Directions: Trace the loops. Then, copy each row.

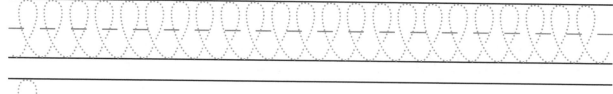

Name: _____ **Date:** _____

Helpful hint:
Little loops, as fun as
can be. That's how we
write the cursive e!

Directions: Trace each letter. Then, practice writing and connecting the letters.

Directions: Trace each letter to finish the words.

ight

eight

b for

before

v n

even

ys

eyes

Name: _____ Date: _____

Directions: Trace each letter. Then, practice writing the letter.

Directions: Trace each letter to finish the names.

Ella

Eli

Eliza

Earl

Name: _____ **Date:** _____

Directions: Trace the loops. Then, color the page.

Name: _____ **Date:** _____

Directions: Trace each letter. Then, write the letters to fill the lines.

d

D

g

y

e

C

Directions: Trace each letter. Then, write the missing letters to complete the words.

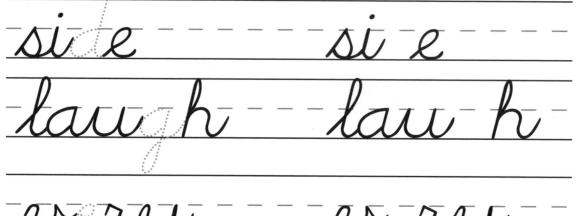

side   *si e*

laugh   *lau h*

very   *v ry*

Name: _____ **Date:** _____

Directions: Trace the loops. Then, copy each row twice.

Name: _____ Date: _____

Helpful hint:
Taller loops are super swell. That's how we write the cursive *l*.

Directions: Trace each letter. Then, practice writing and connecting the letters.

Directions: Trace each letter to finish the words.

left

left

light

light

small

only

Cursive Lowercase

Name: _____ **Date:** _____

Directions: Trace each letter. Then, practice writing the letter.

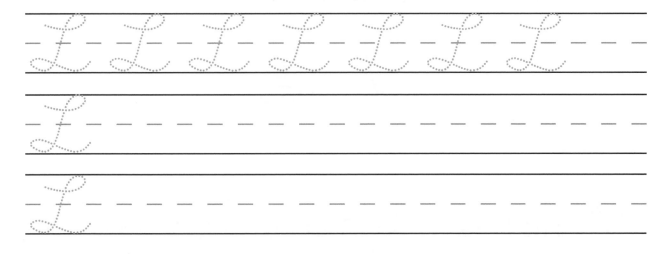

Directions: Trace each letter to finish the names.

Lana

Leti

Leo

Leroy

Name: _____ Date: _____

Directions: Fill in the missing letters.

Which vegetable should you not invite on a boat trip?

____ __ *l* __ *k*

What is a kitten's favorite dessert?

mi ____ *r am*

I am a cat from Africa with a large mane of hair. What am I?

____ __ *ion*

Name: _____ Date: _____

Directions: Trace each letter. Then, write the letters to fill the lines.

Review

_t_

_L_

_a_

_a_

_g_

_g_

Directions: Trace each letter. Then, write the missing letters to complete the words.

one   one

always   lways

good   ood

Name: _____ Date: _____

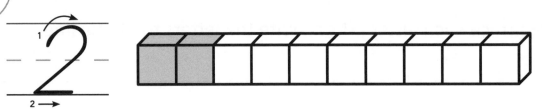

Directions: Trace the number. Then, practice writing 2 on the lines.

Name: _____ **Date:** _____

Directions: Trace each number. Then, practice writing the numbers.

Name: _____ **Date:** _____

Directions: Count how many things you see. Then, write the numbers on the lines.

There are

_____

_____ *cubes.*

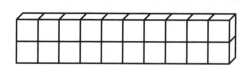

There are

_____

_____ *apples.*

There are

_____

_____ *wheels.*

I have

_____

_____ *cents.*

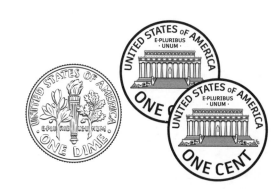

Name: _____ **Date:** _____

Directions: Find and circle the listed words.

n b l s f a a i y l
o u a k b i g x u f
x b h a t m e c s i
j t j y l e a p u p
g a u x f a d d w c
l e g l a d h t k o
b k i c c z s f i t
q m s a s v u a i p
m p w g q h l w y u
z z o e g g y d a d

add   age   cage
dad   egg   glad   leg

Review

Name: _____   Date: _____

Directions: Trace each letter. Then, write the letters to fill the lines.

a

a

l

e

t

L

Directions: Trace each letter. Then, write the missing letters to complete the words.

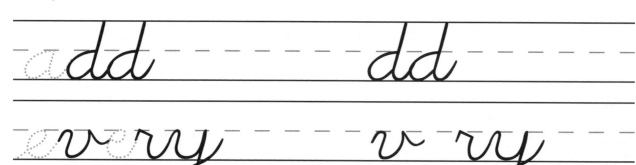

Name: _____ **Date:** _____

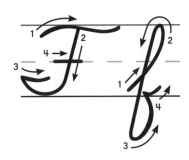

Directions: Trace the loops and curves. Then, copy each row.

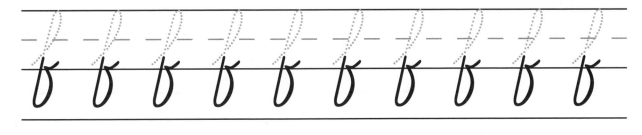

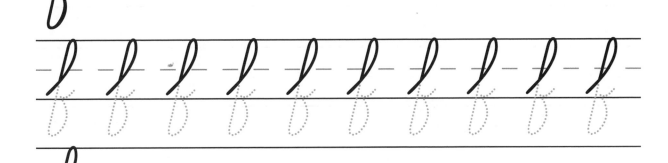

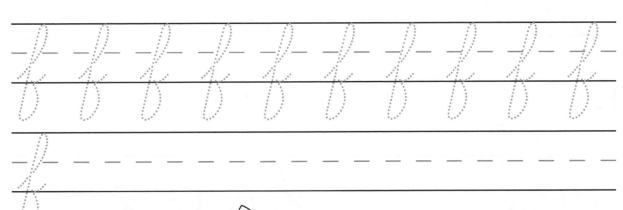

Name: _____ Date: _____

Cursive Lowercase

Directions: Trace each letter. Then, practice writing and connecting the letters.

Directions: Trace each letter to finish the words.

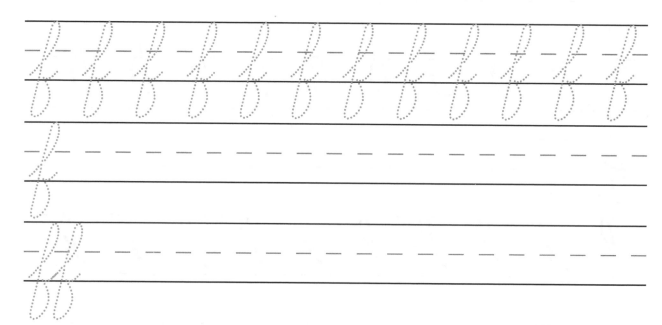

ast

fast

a ff

off

irst

first

be ore

before

130195—180 Days of Cursive: Beginning

Name: _____ **Date:** _____

Directions: Trace each letter. Then, practice writing the letter.

Directions: Trace each letter to finish the names.

Fred

Frank

Frida

Flor

Name: _____ **Date:** _____

Directions: Use the key to match the letters to the numbers.

a	b	c	d	e	f	g	h	i	j	k	l	m
1	2	3	4	5	6	7	8	9	10	11	12	13

n	o	p	q	r	s	t	u	v	w	x	y	z
14	15	16	17	18	19	20	21	22	23	24	25	26

Activity

_____

- - - - - - -

_____

12 9 6 5

_____

- - -

_____

9 6

_____

- - - - - - -

_____

6 5 12 12

_____

- - - - - - -

_____

7 12 1 4

130195—180 Days of Cursive: Beginning

© Shell Education

Name: _____ **Date:** _____

Directions: Trace each letter. Then, write the letters to fill the lines.

Directions: Trace each letter. Then, write the missing letters to complete the names.

bby   *bby*

ave   *ave*

ina   *ina*

Name: _____ Date: _____

Directions: Trace the loops, curves, and letters. Then, copy each row.

Name: _____ **Date:** _____

Helpful hint:
To make the *h*, go up and loop down. Then, bounce up to come back to the ground.

Directions: Trace each letter. Then, practice writing and connecting the letters.

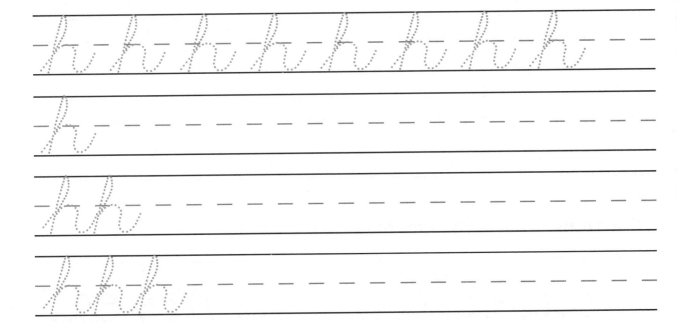

Directions: Trace each letter to finish the words.

hard

high

head

both

Name: _____ Date: _____

Directions: Trace each letter. Then, practice writing the letters.

Directions: Trace each letter to finish the names.

Hawai'i

Humberto

Hannah

Haley

Name: _____ **Date:** _____

Directions: Unscramble the letters. Then, write the words in cursive.

Clue: *Animals*

| lepehnta | _____ ph__nt |

| dqo | _____ |

| ckeinhc | ____ i __ k __ n |
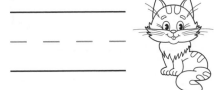

| ogat | ____ t ____ |

| cta | _____ |

| ealeg | _____ |

© Shell Education

Activity

Name: _____ Date: _____

Directions: Trace each letter. Then, write the letters to fill the lines.

h

H

g

y

e

E

Directions: Trace each letter. Then, write the missing letters to complete the words.

add   *a___*

girl   *___irl*

every   *___very*

Name: _____ **Date:** _____

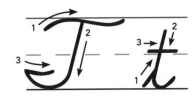

Directions: Trace the curved lines. Then, copy each row.

Name: _____ Date: _____

Helpful hint:
You will need these steps to make a *t*. Up, down, and then across. It's as easy as 1, 2, 3!

Directions: Trace each letter. Then, practice writing and connecting the letters.

Directions: Trace each letter to finish the words.

tell

tell

little

little

think

think

cat

cat

Name: _____ **Date:** _____

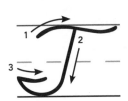 

Directions: Trace each letter. Then, practice writing the letters.

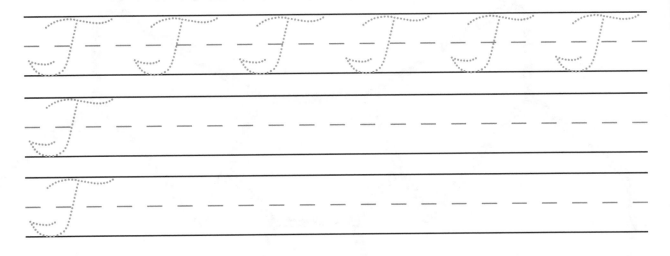

Directions: Trace each letter to finish the names.

Ted

Theo

Tahn

Tasha

Cursive Uppercase

Name: _____ **Date:** _____

Directions: Trace the loops and curves. Then, color the page.

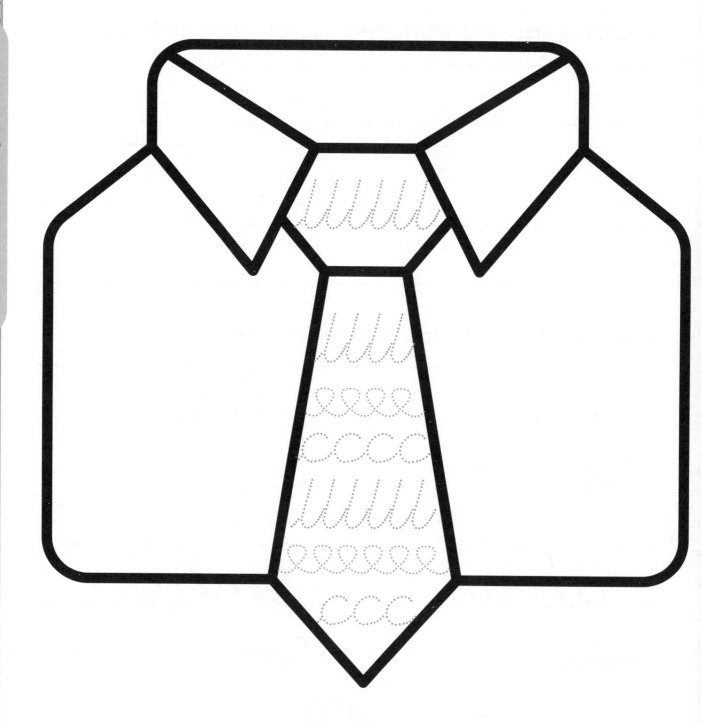

Name: _____ **Date:** _____

Directions: Trace each letter. Then, write the letters to fill the lines.

Directions: Trace each letter. Then, write the words.

Name: _____ Date: _____

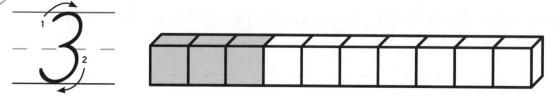

Directions: Trace the number. Then, practice writing 3 on the lines.

Directionality and Strokes

Name: _____ **Date:** _____

Directions: Trace each number. Then, practice writing the numbers.

© Shell Education   130195—180 Days of Cursive: Beginning   69

Numbers

Name: _____ **Date:** _____

Directions: Count how many things you see. Then, write the numbers on the lines.

There are
_____
cubes.

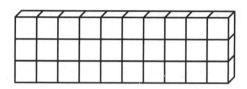

There are
_____
apples.

There are
_____
wheels.

I have
_____
cents.

Name: _____ **Date:** _____

Directions: Fill in the missing letters.

What falls but never gets hurt?

_t e   r   n_

What kind of garden does a baker have?

_a   f   ur_

_g   r   n._

How do turtles call each other?

she   p   on   s

Name: _____ Date: _____

Directions: Trace each letter. Then, write the letters to fill the lines.

Directions: Trace each letter. Then, write the words.

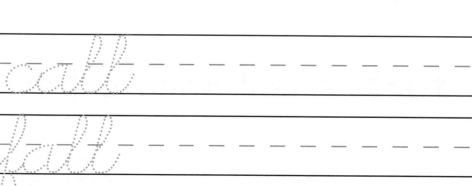

130195—180 Days of Cursive: Beginning

© Shell Education

Name: _____ **Date:** _____

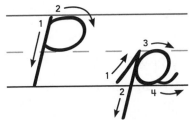

Directions: Trace the curves and lines. Then, copy each row.

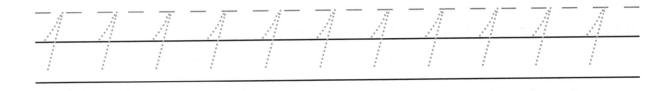

Directionality and Strokes

Name: _____ Date: _____

Helpful hint:
Go down, then up and you will see. Looping around and then out creates the letter *p*!

Directions: Trace each letter. Then, practice writing and connecting the letters.

p p p p p p p p p p

p

p p

p p p

Directions: Trace each letter to finish the words.

page

page

paper

paper

pull

pull

open

open

Name: _____ **Date:** _____

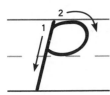 

Directions: Trace each letter. Then, practice writing the letters.

P-P-P-P-P-P-P-P-

P

P

Directions: Trace each letter to finish the names.

Pam

Pam

Peter

Peter

Paige

Paige

Pablo

Pablo

Name: _____ **Date:** _____

Directions: Solve each puzzle by writing the missing letters.

brok n

romis

PROMISE

 +

ha y

tri

round

the world

Name: _____ **Date:** _____

Directions: Trace each letter. Then, write the letters to fill the lines.

_p_

_P_

_t_

_F_

_h_

_H_

Directions: Trace each letter. Then, write the words.

tell

help

Name: _____   Date: _____

Directions: Trace the curves and letters. Then, copy each row.

Name: _____ Date: _____

Helpful hint:
The cursive u is just like print. Up, down, connect. You get the hint!

Directions: Trace each letter. Then, practice writing and connecting the letters.

Directions: Trace each letter to finish the words.

upon

upon

us

hurt

hurt

thought

thought

Name: _____ Date: _____

Cursive Uppercase

Directions: Trace each letter. Then, practice writing the letter.

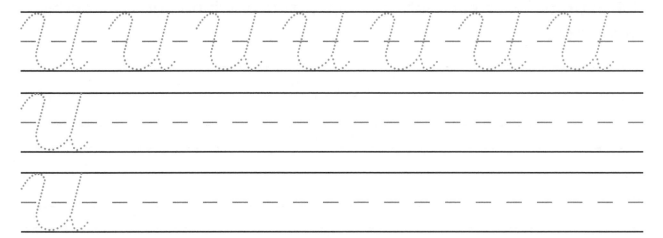

Directions: Trace each letter to finish the names.

Uma

Ulysses

Ursula

Uriel

Name: _____ **Date:** _____

Directions: Use the key to match the letters to the numbers.

a	b	c	d	e	f	g	h	i	j	k	l	m
1	2	3	4	5	6	7	8	9	10	11	12	13

n	o	p	q	r	s	t	u	v	w	x	y	z
14	15	16	17	18	19	20	21	22	23	24	25	26

_____

- - - - - - - - - - -

_____

16   1   16   5   18

_____

- - - - - - - - - - -

_____

16   1   7   5

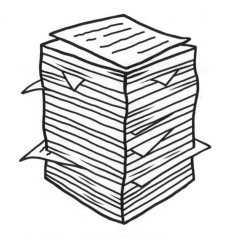

_____

- - - - - - - - - - -

_____

16   21   20

_____

- - - - - - - - - - -

_____

20   8   15   21   7   8   20

Name: _____ **Date:** _____

Directions: Trace each letter. Then, write the letters to fill the lines.

Review

Directions: Trace each letter. Then, write the words.

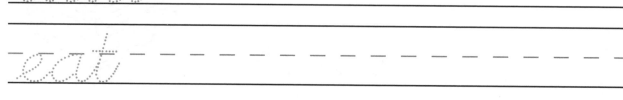

Name: _____ **Date:** _____

Directions: Trace the number. Then, practice writing 4 on the lines.

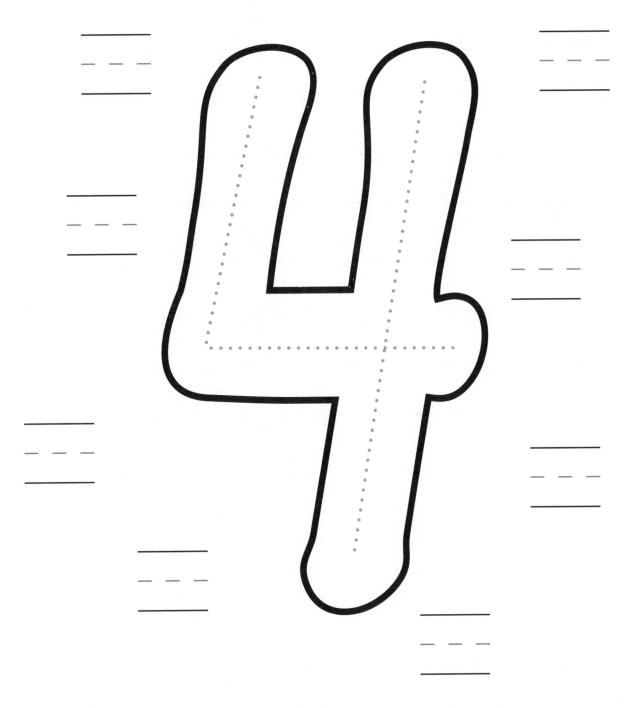

Directionality and Strokes

Name: _____ **Date:** _____

Directions: Trace each number. Then, practice writing the numbers.

0 — — — — — — — — — —   5 — — — — — — — — — —

1 — — — — — — — — — —   6 — — — — — — — — — —

2 — — — — — — — — — —   7 — — — — — — — — — —

3 — — — — — — — — — —   8 — — — — — — — — — —

— — — — — — — — — — —   9 — — — — — — — — — —

Name: _____ **Date:** _____

Directions: Count how many things you see. Then, write the numbers on the lines.

There are
_____
_____ *cubes.*

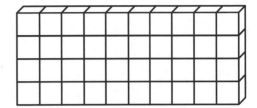

There are
_____
_____ *apples.*

There are
_____
_____ *wheels.*

I have
_____
_____ *cents.*

Name: _____ **Date:** _____

Directions: Trace the lines and curves. Then, color the page.

Activity

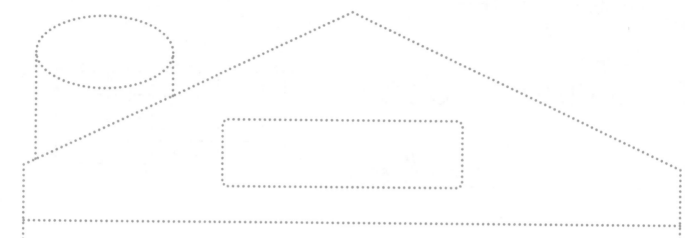

Name: _____ **Date:** _____

Directions: Trace each letter. Then, write the letters to fill the lines.

h

H

t

F

p

P

Directions: Trace each letter. Then, write the words.

face

feet

Name: _____ Date: _____

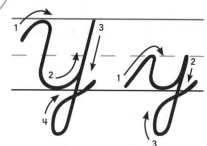

Directions: Trace the curved lines, loops, and letters. Then, copy each row.

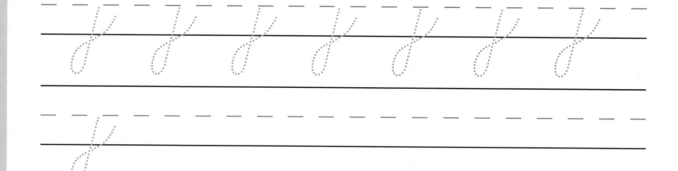

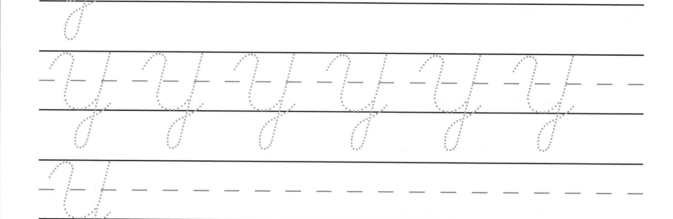

Name: _____   **Date:** _____

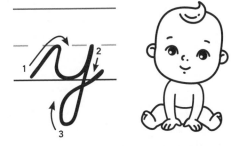

Helpful hint:
Print and cursive y are almost the same. Connecting to other letters is the name of the game!

Directions: Trace each letter. Then, practice writing and connecting the letters.

y y y y y y y y y y

y

y y

Directions: Trace each letter to finish the words.

years

years

try

try

young

young

study

study

Name: _____ **Date:** _____

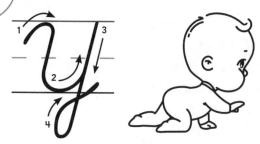

Directions: Trace each letter. Then, practice writing the letter.

Cursive Uppercase

Directions: Trace each letter to finish the names.

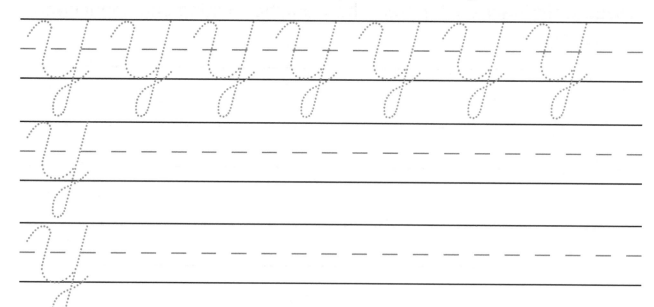

Yaal

Yvonne

Yuri

Yadira

Name: _____ **Date:** _____

Directions: Trace the loops. Then, color the page.

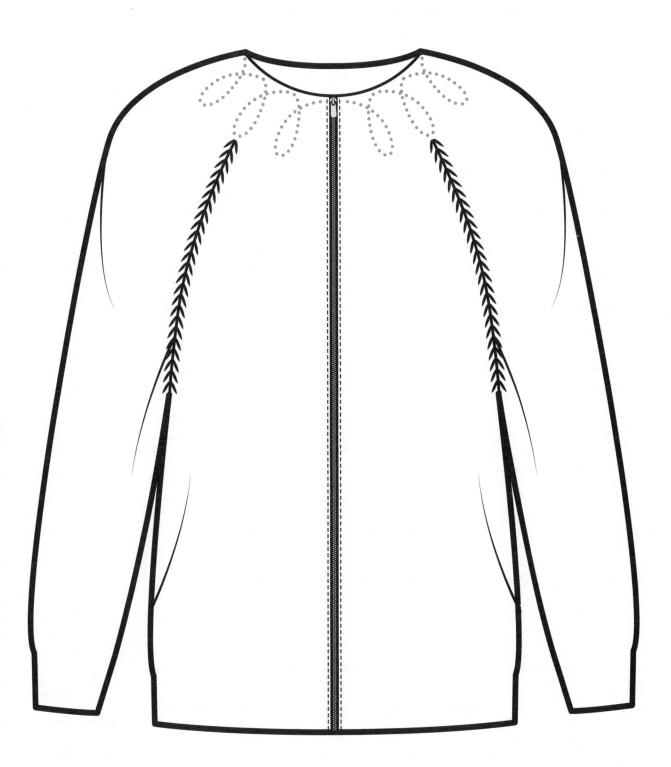

Name: _____ **Date:** _____

Directions: Trace each letter. Then, write the letters to fill the lines.

Review

Directions: Trace each letter. Then, write the words.

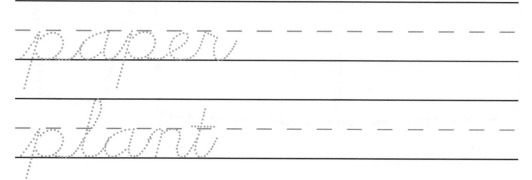

Name: _____   Date: _____

Directions: Trace the letters. Then, copy each row.

Name: _____ Date: _____

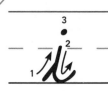

Helpful hint:
Practice returning down on your line. Don't forget the dot and you'll be fine!

Cursive Lowercase

Directions: Trace each letter. Then, practice writing and connecting the letters.

Directions: Trace each letter to finish the words.

if

its

little

point

© Shell Education

Name: _____ **Date:** _____

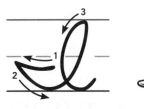 

Directions: Trace each letter. Then, practice writing the letter.

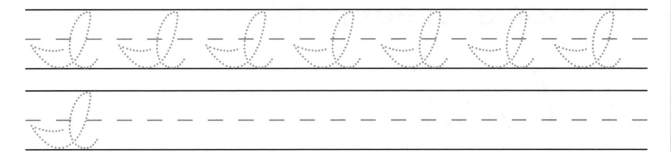

Directions: Trace each letter to finish the names.

Izzy

Isaiah

Isaac

Isla

Cursive Uppercase

Name: _____   **Date:** _____

Directions: Fill in the missing letterss.

What is so fragile that saying its name breaks it?

s l nc

What has a head and tail but no body?

a co n

What gets sharper the more you use it?

our br n

© Shell Education

Name: _____ **Date:** _____

Directions: Trace each letter. Then, write the letters to fill the lines.

Directions: Trace each letter. Then, write the words.

Name: _____ **Date:** _____

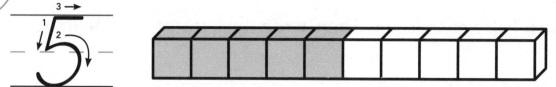

Directions: Trace the number. Then, practice writing 5 on the lines.

Name: _____   **Date:** _____

Directions: Trace each number. Then, practice writing the numbers.

50 — — — — — — — — — —   55 — — — — — — — — — —

51 — — — — — — — — — —   56 — — — — — — — — — —

52 — — — — — — — — — —   57 — — — — — — — — — —

53 — — — — — — — — — —   58 — — — — — — — — — —

54 — — — — — — — — — —   59 — — — — — — — — — —

Numbers

Name: _____   **Date:** _____

Directions: Count how many things you see. Then, write the numbers on the lines.

There are
_____
_____ *cubes.*

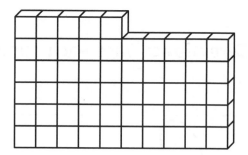

There are
_____
_____ *apples.*

There are
_____
_____ *wheels.*

I have
_____
_____ *cents.*

130195—180 Days of Cursive: Beginning

Name: _____ **Date:** _____

Directions: Connect the dots. Then, color the page.

Name: _____ **Date:** _____

Directions: Trace each number. Then, write the numbers to fill the lines.

1
_____

2
_____

3
_____

4
_____

5
_____

Directions: Trace each letter. Then, write the words.

at
_____

the
_____

Name: _____ **Date:** _____

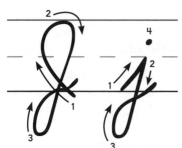

Directions: Trace the curved lines and letters. Then, copy each row.

Directionality and Strokes

Name: _____   Date: _____

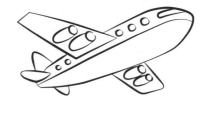

Helpful hint:

Up, then down below the line. Don't forget the dot and your *j* will be fine!

Cursive Lowercase

Directions: Trace each letter. Then, practice writing and connecting the letters.

Directions: Trace each letter to finish the words.

just

just

jacket

jacket

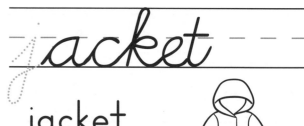

jump

jump

jet

jet

Name: _____   **Date:** _____

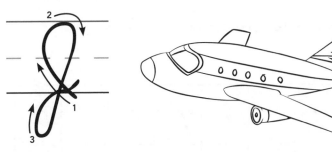

Directions: Trace each letter. Then, practice writing the letters.

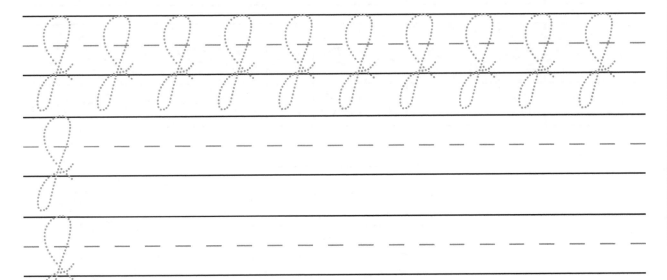

Directions: Trace each letter to finish the names.

June

June

Jessie

Jessie

July

July

James

James

Name: _____ Date: _____

Directions: Use the key to match the letters to the numbers.

a	b	c	d	e	f	g	h	i	j	k	l	m
1	2	3	4	5	6	7	8	9	10	11	12	13

n	o	p	q	r	s	t	u	v	w	x	y	z
14	15	16	17	18	19	20	21	22	23	24	25	26

Activity

_____

- - - - - - - - - - - - -

_____

10   21   13   16

_____

- - - - - - - - - - - - -

_____

10   21   19   20

_____

- - - - - - - - - - - - -

_____

10   1   13

_____

- - - - - - - - - - - - -

_____

8   1   16   16   25

Name: _____ **Date:** _____

Directions: Trace each letter. Then, write the letters to fill the lines.

and
Go to se
World o
Sell your b

x

y

y

i

t

Directions: Trace each letter. Then, write the words.

big

tell

Name: _____ Date:_____

Directions: Trace the curved lines and letters. Then, copy each row. Notice that the letter *o* ends at the top.

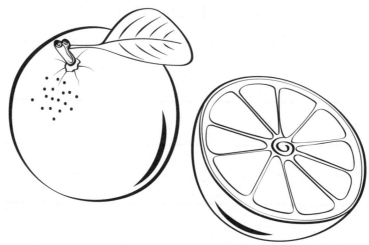

Name: _____ **Date:** _____

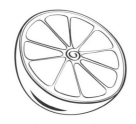

Helpful hint:
Cursive *o* is different. At the end, you don't drop. To get to the next letter, connect from the top!

Directions: Trace each letter. Then, practice writing and connecting the letters.

Directions: Trace each letter to finish the words.

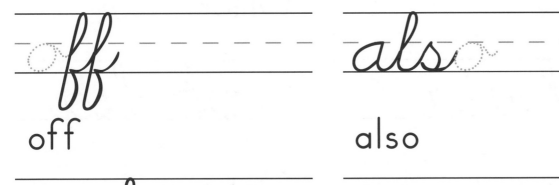

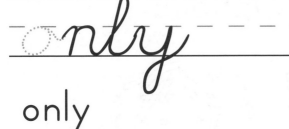

off

also

only

too

Name: _____ **Date:** _____

Directions: Unscramble the letters. Then, write the words in cursive.

Clue: *Food*

bcolirco

br ___ i

ngearo

r ___ g

oolesdn

n ___ d ___ s

rokp

p ___ rk

supo

s ___ up

ocadova

v ___ d

Name: _____ **Date:** _____

Directions: Trace each letter. Then, write the letters to fill the lines.

a

O

i

I

f

f

Directions: Trace each letter. Then, write the words.

old

food

Name: _____   **Date:** _____

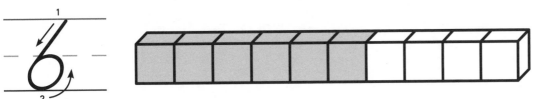

Directions: Trace the number. Then, practice writing 6 on the lines.

Name: _____ **Date:** _____

Directions: Trace each number. Then, practice writing the numbers.

Numbers

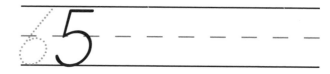

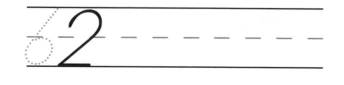

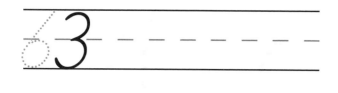

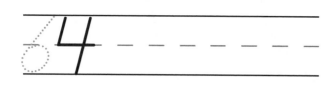

Name: _____ **Date:** _____

Directions: Count how many things you see. Then, write the numbers on the lines.

There are

_____

cubes.

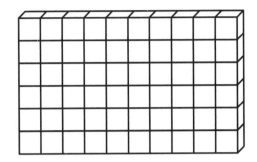

There are

_____

apples.

There are

_____

wheels.

I have

_____

cents.

Activity

Name: _____ Date: _____

Directions: Trace each 6. Then, color the page.

Name: _____ **Date:** _____

Directions: Trace each letter. Then, write the letters to fill the lines.

i

L

j

f

o

O

Directions: Trace each letter. Then, write the words.

too

good

Name: _____   **Date:** _____

Directionality and Strokes

Directions: Trace the curved lines. Then, copy each row.

Name: _____   Date: _____

Helpful hint:
Here is another letter that goes nonstop. Just like the o, connect to other letters from the top!

Directions: Trace each letter. Then, practice writing and connecting the letters.

Directions: Trace each letter to finish the words.

wash

wash

answer

answer

why

why

follow

follow

Name: _____ Date: _____

Directions: Trace each letter. Then, practice writing the letter.

Wᵤ Wᵤ Wᵤ Wᵤ Wᵤ

W

W

Directions: Trace each letter to finish the names.

Wayne

Wayne

William

William

Willow

Willow

Winifred

Winifred

Name: _____ **Date:** _____

Directions: Unscramble the letters. Then, write the words in cursive.

Clue: *animals*

lewah _____ *h* _____

woc _____
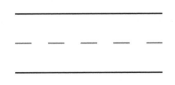

wrom _____ *rm* _____

lfow _____

lrusaw _____ *rus* _____
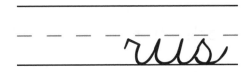

ombatw _____ *mb* _____

Name: _____   Date: _____

Directions: Trace each letter. Then, write the letters to fill the lines.

u

U

o

O

f

g

Directions: Trace each letter. Then, write the words.

well

little

Name: _____ **Date:** _____

Directions: Trace the loops, curved lines, and letters. Then, copy each row.

Name: _____ **Date:** _____

Helpful hint:
Loop up, down, come around and you will see. Connect from the top like the *o* and *w*. That's how we make a cursive *b*!

Directions: Trace each letter. Then, practice writing and connecting the letters.

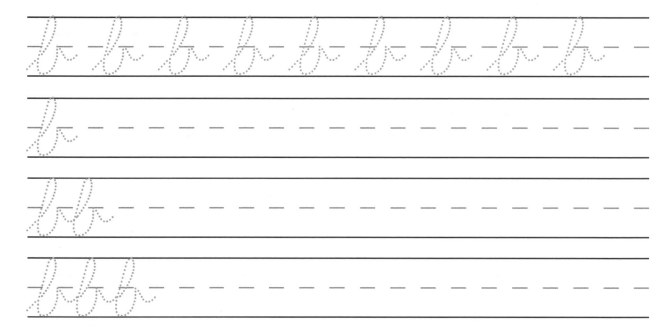

Directions: Trace each letter to finish the words.

because

both

book

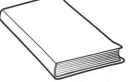

above

Name: _____ **Date:** _____

Directions: Trace each letter. Then, practice writing the letter.

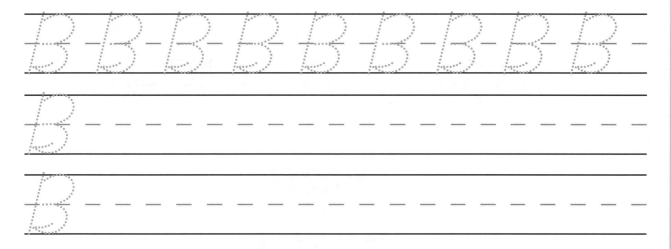

Directions: Trace each letter to finish the names.

Briseda

Brianna

Ben

Blake

Directions: Solve each puzzle by writing the missing letters.

BAD wolf

_ig _ _d wolf

man
board

m _ n _ _ v _ r _ _rd

read

_r _ d _ tw _ n

the _ _in _s

Name: _____ Date: _____

Directions: Trace each letter. Then, write the letters to fill the lines.

Directions: Trace each letter. Then, write the words.

Name: _____ **Date:** _____

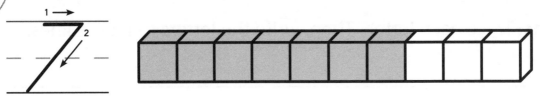

Directions: Trace the number. Then, practice writing 7 on the lines.

Name: _____ **Date:** _____

Directions: Trace each number. Then, practice writing the numbers.

0 — — — — — — — —   5 — — — — — — — —

1 — — — — — — — —   6 — — — — — — — —

2 — — — — — — — —   7 — — — — — — — —

3 — — — — — — — —   8 — — — — — — — —

4 — — — — — — — —   9 — — — — — — — —

Numbers

Name: _____ **Date:** _____

Directions: Count how many things you see. Then, write the numbers on the lines.

$\mathcal{T}here\ are$

_____

_____ cubes.

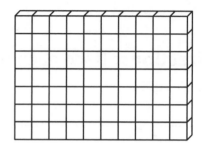

$\mathcal{T}here\ are$

_____

_____ apples.

$\mathcal{T}here\ are$

_____

_____ wheels.

$\mathcal{I}\ have$

_____

_____ cents.

Name: _____ **Date:** _____

Directions: Use the key to match the letters to the numbers.

a	b	c	d	e	f	g	h	i	j	k	l	m
1	2	3	4	5	6	7	8	9	10	11	12	13

n	o	p	q	r	s	t	u	v	w	x	y	z
14	15	16	17	18	19	20	21	22	23	24	25	26

Activity

_____

- - - - - -

_____

12 9 6 5

_____

- - - -

_____

12 20

_____

- - - - -

_____

12 5 20

_____

- - - - - -

_____

12 5 6 20

Name: _____ Date: _____

Directions: Trace each letter. Then, write the letters to fill the lines.

a

C

u

W

k

B

Review

Directions: Trace each letter. Then, write the missing name.

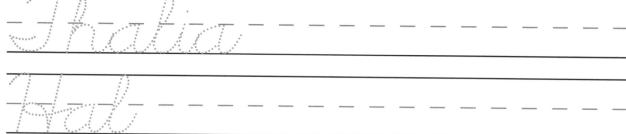

Name: _____ Date: _____

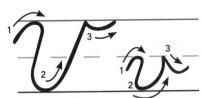

Directions: Trace the letters. Then, copy each row.

Directionality and Strokes

Name: _____ **Date:** _____

Helpful hint:
Like the *o*, *w*, and *b*,
connect from the top
when writing a *v*.

Directions: Trace each letter. Then, practice writing and connecting the letters.

Directions: Trace each letter to finish the words.

very

give

move

over

Name: _____ **Date:** _____

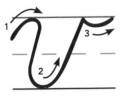 

Directions: Trace each letter. Then, practice writing the letters.

Directions: Trace each letter to finish the names.

Victor

Victor

Violet

Violet

Vince

Vince

Valeria

Valeria

Name: _____ **Date:** _____

Directions: Unscramble the letters. Then, write the words in cursive.

Clue: *sports*

bskatbaell b sk b

ocsrec a r

folltabo ot l

lfog g

selalbab b s a

nneist t nn s

Name: _____ Date: _____

Directions: Trace each letter. Then, write the letters to fill the lines.

Review

Directions: Trace each letter. Then, write the word and name.

Name: _____ **Date:** _____

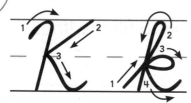

Directions: Trace the loops and curved lines. Then, copy each row.

Name: _____   **Date:** _____

Cursive Lowercase

> **Helpful hint:**
> Up, down, and then halfway up
> to loop around. Take your time and
> practice every day. In no time, you
> will be making the cursive *k*!

Directions: Trace each letter. Then, practice writing and connecting the letters.

k k k k k k k k k k

k

kk

kkk

Directions: Trace each letter to finish the words.

keep

keep

take

take

know

know

think

think

Name: _____ Date: _____

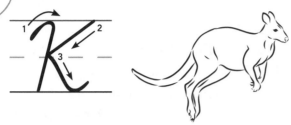

Cursive Uppercase

Directions: Trace each letter. Then, practice writing the letter.

K   K   K   K   K   K   K

K

K

Directions: Trace each letter to finish the names.

Kaia

Kaia

Keisha

Keisha

Kayden

Kayden

Kai

Kai

Name: _____ **Date:** _____

Directions: Trace the sentence. Then, color the page.

Katie keeps

ketchup in the

kitchen.

Name: _____ Date: _____

Directions: Trace each letter. Then, write the letters to fill the lines.

b

B

v

V

k

K

Directions: Trace each letter. Then, write the word and name.

keep

Kayla

Name: _____ **Date:** _____

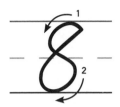 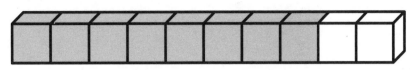

Directions: Trace the number. Then, practice writing 8 on the lines.

130195—180 Days of Cursive: Beginning

Name: _____ **Date:** _____

Directions: Trace each number. Then, practice writing the numbers.

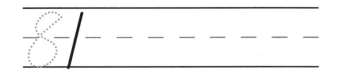

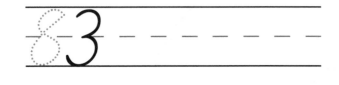

Name: _____ **Date:** _____

Directions: Count how many things you see. Then, write the numbers on the lines.

There are

_____

_____ *cubes.*

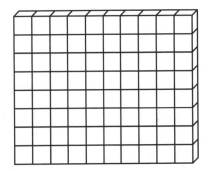

There are

_____

_____ *apples.*

There are

_____

_____ *wheels.*

I have

_____

_____ *cents.*

130195—180 Days of Cursive: Beginning

Activity

Name: _____ **Date:** _____

Directions: Connect the dots. Then, color the page.

130195—180 Days of Cursive: Beginning   © Shell Education

Name: _____ Date: _____

Directions: Trace each letter. Then, write the letters to fill the lines.

g

y

h

B

v

V

Directions: Trace each letter. Then, write the sentence.

I like to eat.

Name: _____   Date: _____

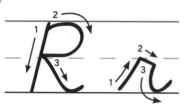

Directions: Trace the lines and letters. Then, copy each row.

Name: _____   **Date:** _____

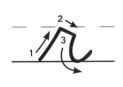

Helpful hint:
A short line up then slant down, not too far. Curve down and come back up to make the *r*.

Directions: Trace each letter. Then, practice writing and connecting the letters.

Directions: Trace each letter to finish the words.

read

right

large

letter

Name: _____ Date: _____

Directions: Trace each letter. Then, practice writing the letters.

R R R R R R R R R R R

R

R

Directions: Trace each letter to finish the names.

Riley

Riley

Reyna

Reyna

Ryan

Ryan

Roland

Roland

Name: _____ **Date:** _____

Directions: Solve each puzzle by writing the missing letters.

no / se

_b kn n s_

_w t f ll_

eggs

—————

easy

ggs v r sy

Activity

Name: _____ **Date:** _____

Directions: Trace each letter. Then, write the letters to fill the lines.

v

V

k

K

r

R

Directions: Trace each letter. Then, write the sentence.

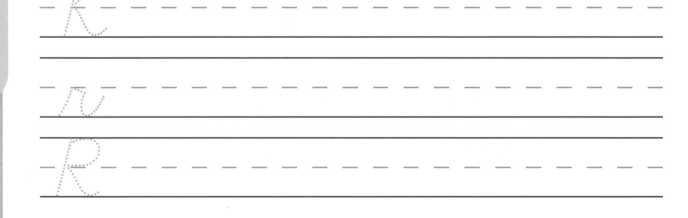

I like to read.

Name: _____ **Date:** _____

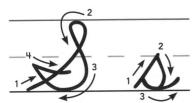

Directions: Trace the curved lines and letters. Then, copy each row.

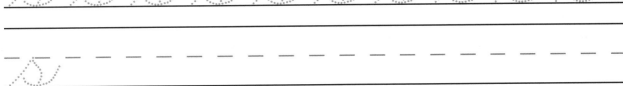

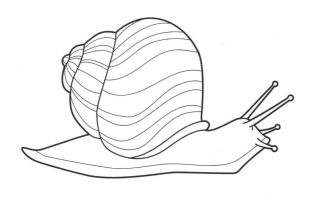
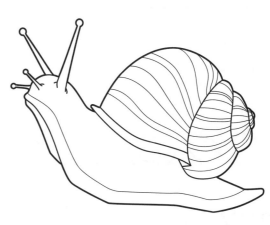

Name: _____ Date: _____

Helpful hint:
Go up, then curve around. Come back out for success. That is how you make the s.

Directions: Trace each letter. Then, practice writing and connecting the letters.

Directions: Trace each letter to finish the words.

ame

same

how

show

because

because

doe

does

Cursive Lowercase

Name: _____ **Date:** _____

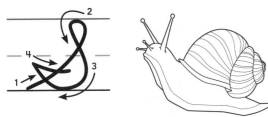

Directions: Trace each letter. Then, practice writing the letter.

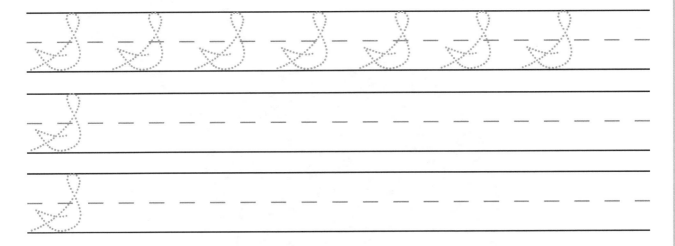

Directions: Trace each letter to finish the names.

amuel

Samuel

tan

Stan

hannon

Shannon

ara

Sara

Name: _____ **Date:** _____

Directions: Trace each letter s. Then, color the page.

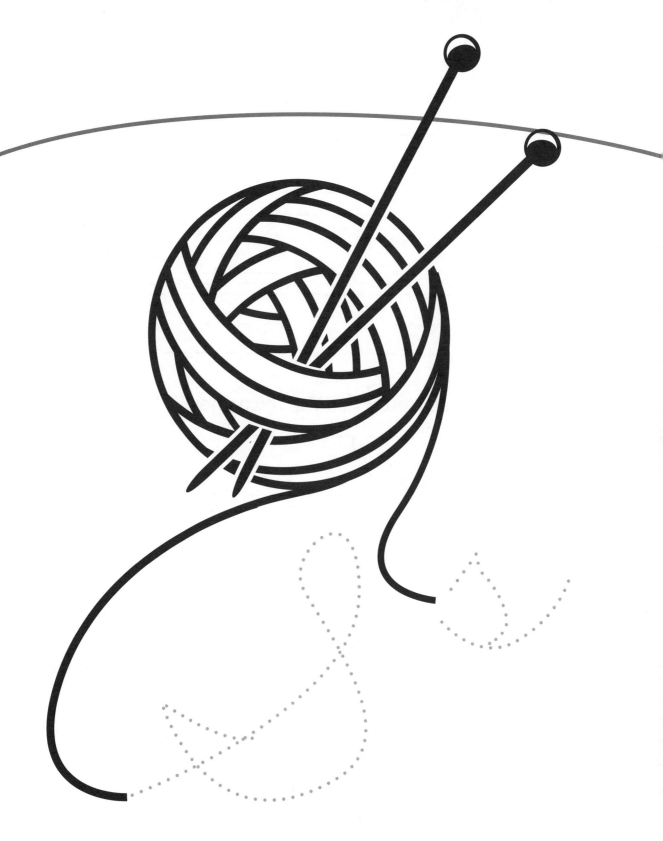

Name: _____ Date: _____

Directions: Trace each letter. Then, write the letters to fill the lines.

Directions: Trace each letter. Then, write the sentence.

I see a cat

Name: _____ **Date:** _____

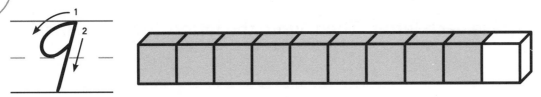

Directions: Trace the number. Then, practice writing 9 on the lines.

Name: _____ **Date:** _____

9

Directions: Trace each number. Then, practice writing the numbers.

90 _ _ _ _ _ _ _ _ _ _ _   95 _ _ _ _ _ _ _ _ _ _ _

91 _ _ _ _ _ _ _ _ _ _ _   96 _ _ _ _ _ _ _ _ _ _ _

92 _ _ _ _ _ _ _ _ _ _ _   97 _ _ _ _ _ _ _ _ _ _ _

93 _ _ _ _ _ _ _ _ _ _ _   98 _ _ _ _ _ _ _ _ _ _ _

94 _ _ _ _ _ _ _ _ _ _ _   99 _ _ _ _ _ _ _ _ _ _ _

Name: _____ **Date:** _____

Directions: Count how many things you see. Then, write the numbers on the lines.

There are _____ *cubes.*

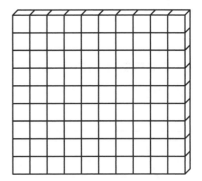

There are _____ *apples.*

There are _____ *wheels.*

I have _____ *cents.*

Activity

Name: _____ **Date:** _____

Directions: Unscramble the letters. Then, write the words in cursive.

Clue: Nature

eesrt

_r_ _s_

orcsk

_r_ _c_

iersvr

_r_ _e_ _s_

snniehsu

_u_ _s_ _n_

rssag

_g_

nailsam

_n_ _m_ _s_

Name: _____ **Date:** _____

Directions: Trace each letter. Then, write the letters to fill the lines.

Review

f

F

r

R

s

S

Directions: Trace each letter. Then, finish the sentence.

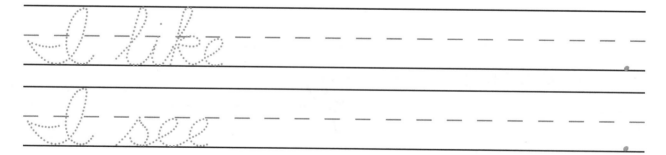

I like

I see

Name: _____ **Date:** _____

Directionality and Strokes

Directions: Trace the letters and curved lines. Then, copy each row.

Name: _____   **Date:** _____

Helpful hint:
To make the *n*, you curve up again. Connect from the bottom and this letter is your friend!

Cursive Lowercase

Directions: Trace each letter. Then, practice writing and connecting the letters.

n n n n n n n n n

n

n n

n n n

Directions: Trace each letter to finish the words.

name

name

only

only

need

need

often

often

Name: _____ **Date:** _____

Directions: Trace each letter. Then, practice writing the letter.

Directions: Trace each letter to finish the names.

Nia

Nia

Nany

Newton

Newton

Nick

Nick

Name: _____ Date: _____

Directions: Trace the curves and letters. Then, color the page.

Name: _____ **Date:** _____

Directions: Trace each letter. Then, write the letters to fill the lines.

A

R

S

J

N

A

Directions: Trace each letter. Then, finish the sentences.

She goes

They are

Name: _____ **Date:** _____

Directions: Trace the letters and curves. Then, copy each row.

Directionality and Strokes

Name: _____ **Date:** _____

Helpful hint:
Just like the *n*, you curve up again and again. Connect from the bottom to make the *m*.

Directions: Trace each letter. Then, practice writing and connecting the letters.

m m m m m m m

m

mm

mmm

Directions: Trace each letter to finish the words.

means

means

same

same

might

might

seem

seem

Cursive Lowercase

Cursive Uppercase

Name: _____   Date: _____

Directions: Trace each letter. Then, practice writing the letter.

$\mathcal{M}$ $\mathcal{M}$ $\mathcal{M}$ $\mathcal{M}$ $\mathcal{M}$ $\mathcal{M}$ $\mathcal{M}$ $\mathcal{M}$

$\mathcal{M}$

$\mathcal{M}$

Directions: Trace each letter to finish the names.

Maria

Maria

Molly

Molly

Mike

Mike

Manuel

Manuel

Name: _____ **Date:** _____

Directions: Trace the sentence. Then, color the page.

Miriam made mini

mango muffins

for Manny.

Name: _____ Date: _____

Directions: Trace each letter. Then, write the letters to fill the lines.

Review

_____
- -
s
_____

_____
- -
y
_____

_____
- -
n
_____

_____
- -
h
_____

_____
- -
m
_____

_____
- -
n
_____

Directions: Trace each letter. Then, finish the sentences.

_____
I went - - - - - - - - - - - - - - - - - .
_____

_____
I love - - - - - - - - - - - - - - - - - .
_____

Name: _____ Date: _____

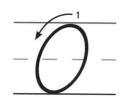 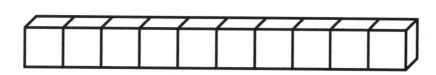

Directions: Trace the number. Then, practice writing 0 on the lines.

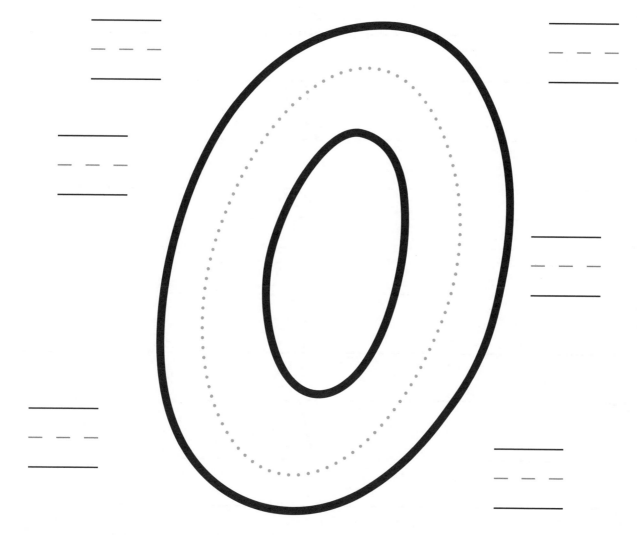

Name: _____ **Date:** _____

Directions: Trace each number. Then, practice writing the numbers.

Numbers

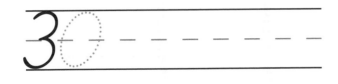

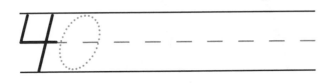

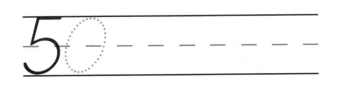

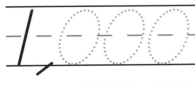

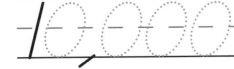

Name: _____ **Date:** _____

Directions: Count how many things you see. Then, write the numbers on the lines.

There are

_____

cubes.

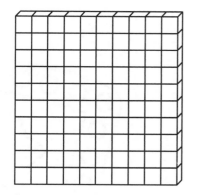

There are

_____

apples.

There are

_____

wheels.

I have

_____

cents.

Name: _____ **Date:** _____

Directions: Trace the times. Then, color the picture.

The Funny
Movie
Showtimes:
1:00, 3:35
5:15, 7:00

Name: _____ **Date:** _____

Directions: Trace each number. Then, write the numbers to fill the lines.

6

7

8

9

10

Directions: Trace each letter. Then, finish the sentences.

She goes

They are

Review

Name: _____ **Date:** _____

Directions: Trace the letters and lines. Then, copy each row.

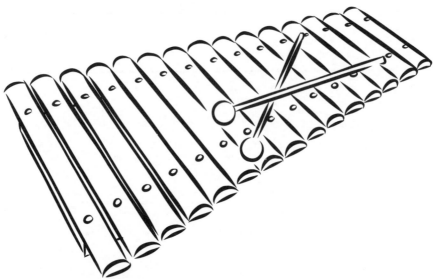

Name: _____ **Date:** _____

Helpful hint:
To make the *x*, you curve up and then down. Lift your pencil to cross, no need to frown!

Directions: Trace each letter. Then, practice writing and connecting the letters.

Directions: Trace each letter to finish the words.

x-ray

x-ray

T-Rex

T-Rex

xylophone

xylophone

next

next

Name: _____ Date: _____

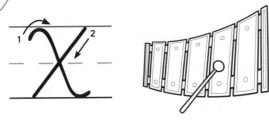

Cursive Uppercase

Directions: Trace each letter. Then, practice writing the letter.

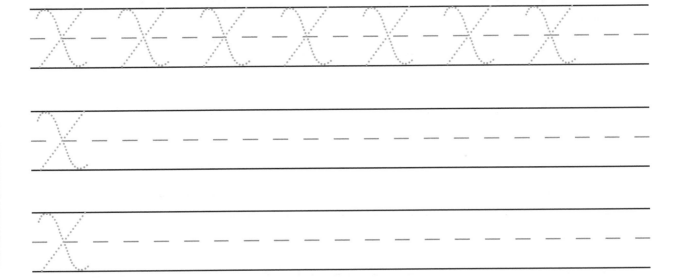

Directions: Trace each letter to finish the names.

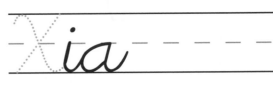

Xiomara

Xavia

Xian

Xia

© Shell Education

Name: _____ **Date:** _____

Directions: Trace the *X*. Then, color the page.

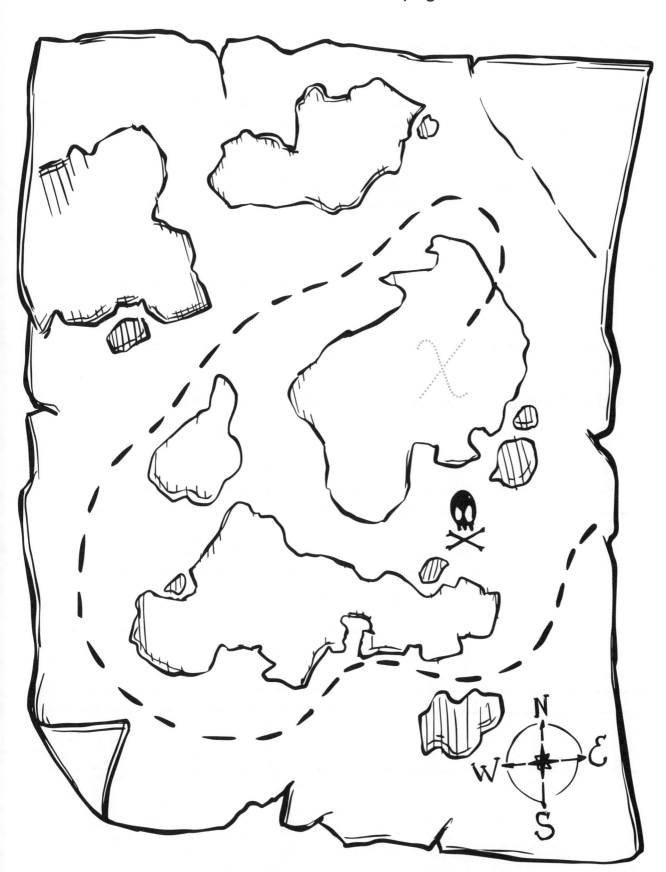

Activity

Name: _____ **Date:** _____

Directions: Trace each letter. Then, write the letters to fill the lines.

n

N

n

N

Directions: Trace each letter. Then, write the sentence.

Where do you

live?

Name: _____ **Date:** _____

Directions: Trace the curves, lines, and letters. Then, copy each row.

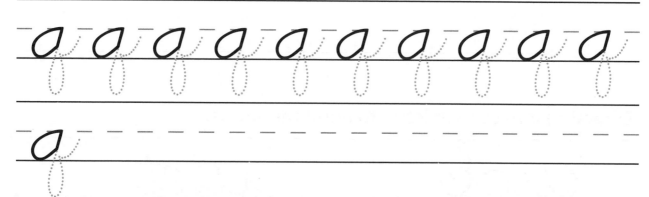

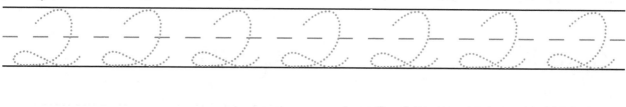

Name: _____ Date: _____

_____

Helpful hint:
To make the *q*, you start with
an *a*. Just keep going below the line,
curve back, and bounce up.
That's the way!

Directions: Trace each letter. Then, practice writing
and connecting the letters.

Directions: Trace each letter to finish the words.

quick

quick

quiet

quiet

queen

queen

quarter

quarter

Name: _____ **Date:** _____

Directions: Trace each letter. Then, practice writing the letter.

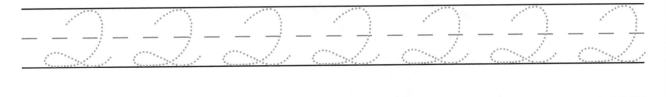

Directions: Trace each letter to finish the names.

Quill

Quincy

Quinton

Quinn

Name: _____ **Date:** _____

Directions: Trace the sentence. Then, color the page.

Quincy quietly

completes a quiz.

Name: _____ **Date:** _____

Directions: Trace each letter. Then, write the letters to fill the lines.

X

X

q

2

Directions: Trace each letter. Then, answer the question.

Who is the quietest

person you know?

Name: _____ Date: _____

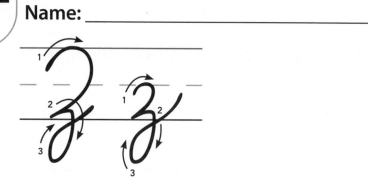

Directions: Trace the curves and letters. Then, copy each row.

Name: _____

Date: _____

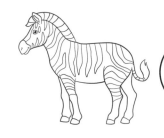

Helpful hint:
Curve up and down, drop below the line, you see. Then loop back up and come around to make the cursive z.

Directions: Trace each letter. Then, practice writing and connecting the letters.

Directions: Trace each letter to finish the words.

zebra

zebra

zoo

zoo

zipper

zipper

jazz

jazz

Cursive Lowercase

Name: _____ Date: _____

Cursive Uppercase

Directions: Trace each letter. Then, practice writing the letter.

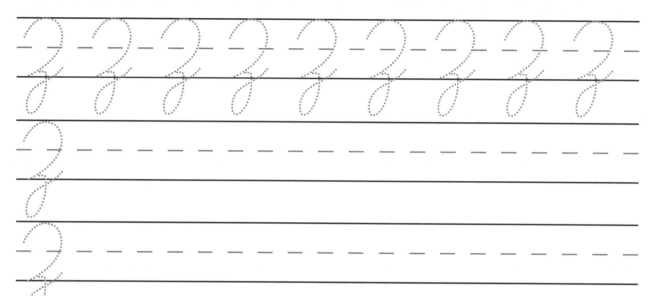

Directions: Trace each letter to finish the names.

Zara

Zara

Zoe

Zoe

Zach

Zach

Zane

Zane

Name: _____ **Date:** _____

Directions: Trace the lines. Then, color the page.

The quick brown

fox jumps over

the lazy dog.

Name: _____ **Date:** _____

Directions: Trace each letter. Then, write the letters to fill the lines.

Review

Directions: Read the sentence. Then, write the sentence in cursive.

The quick brown fox jumps over the lazy dog.

Lowercase Letter Guide

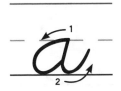    

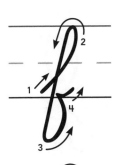   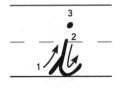 

 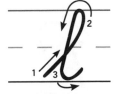   

   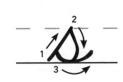 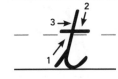

Uppercase Letter Guide

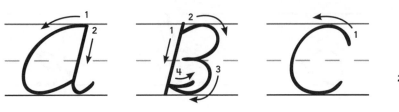
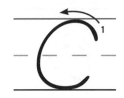

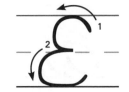

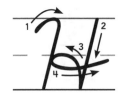
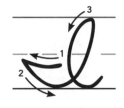
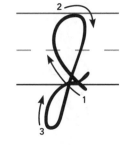

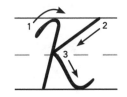

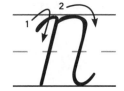
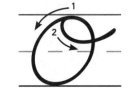

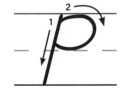

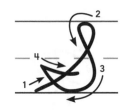
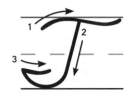

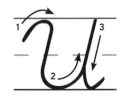
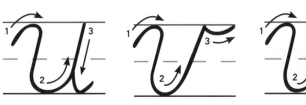
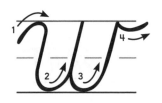

Number Guide

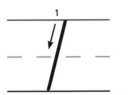

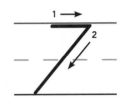
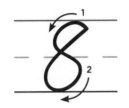

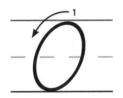

Practice Lines

Answer Key

There are many open-ended pages and writing prompts in this book. For those activities, the answers will vary. Examples are given as needed.

Week 2 Day 4 (page 21)

a clock

a catfish

a carrot

Week 3 Day 4 (page 26)

Week 4 Day 4 (page 31)

cat

dog

duck

Week 5 Day 4 (page 36)

carrot

grape

orange

apple

kale

banana

Week 7 Day 4 (page 46)

a leek

mice cream

a lion

Week 8 Day 4 (page 51)

Answer Key *(cont.)*

Week 9 Day 4 (page 56)

life

if

fell

glad

Week 10 Day 4 (page 61)

elephant

dog

chicken

goat

cat

eagle

Week 12 Day 4 (page 71)

the rain

a flour garden

shell phones

Week 13 Day 4 (page 76)

broken promise

happy

trip around the world

Week 14 Day 4 (page 81)

paper

page

put

thought

Week 17 Day 4 (page 96)

silence

a coin

your brain

Week 19 Day 4 (page 106)

jump

just

jam

happy

Week 20 Day 4 (page 111)

broccoli

orange

noodles

pork

soup

avocado

Answer Key *(cont.)*

Week 22 Day 4 (page 121)

whale

cow

worm

wolf

walrus

wombat

Week 23 Day 4 (page 126)

big bad wolf

man overboard

read between the lines

Week 24 Day 4 (page 131)

life

it

let

left

Week 25 Day 4 (page 136)

basketball

soccer

football

golf

baseball

tennis

Week 28 Day 4 (page 151)

broken nose

waterfall

eggs over easy

Week 30 Day 4 (page 161)

trees

rocks

rivers

sunshine

grass

animals

Suggested Websites

Website Title	Address	Content
ABC Mouse	www.abcmouse.com	alphabet, phonics
Learning A–Z	www.learninga-z.com	alphabet, phonics
Student Handouts	www.studenthandouts.com	alphabet

Digital Resources

Accessing the Digital Resources

The digital resources can be downloaded by following these steps:

1. Go to **www.tcmpub.com/digital**
2. Use the ISBN number to redeem the digital resources.
3. Respond to the question using the book.
4. Follow the prompts on the Content Cloud website to sign in or create a new account.
5. The redeemed content will now be on your My Content screen. Click on the product to look through the Digital Resources. All files can be downloaded, while some files can also be previewed, opened, and shared.

   - Please note: Some files provided for download have large file sizes. Download times for these larger files vary based on your download speed.

Contents of the Digital Resources
Activities

- Hands-on practice for writing uppercase and lowercase letters
- Sentence-writing practice
- Handwriting lines for printing activities